JAMAICA

AF767157

PEP

Language Arts

Performance Task

GRADE 6

Practice Papers

hachette LEARNING

The Publishers would like to thank the following for permission to reproduce copyright material.

Photo credits

t = top, b = below, l = left, r = right, c = centre, b/g = background

p.7: (t) © Rolf Nussbaumer/Danita Delimont/stock.adobe.com, (tl) © Blogtrip/stock.adobe.com, (cr) © steheap/stock.adobe.com, (bl) © Janusz Pienkowski/Shutterstock.com, (b) © Turgut/stock.adobe.com; p.8: (l) © Georgios Kollidas/stock.adobe.com, (r) © Janusz Pienkowski/Shutterstock.com; p.22: © Prachaya Roekdeethaweesab/Shutterstock.com; p.34: © bogdanserban/stock.adobe.com; p.42: © matiasdelcarmine/stock.adobe.com; p.50: (t) © Prostock-studio/stock.adobe.com, (b) © AnnaStills/stock.adobe.com; p.51: (t) © Rawpixel.com/stock.adobe.com, (c) © sborisov/stock.adobe.com.
p. 42: 'Rain' @ Valerie Bloom.

We have used all reasonable efforts to correctly credit all licensed material in this book. If your material has been mis-credited please contact us so that we can amend the credit for future editions.

Acknowledgements

Although every effort has been made to ensure that website addresses are correct at time of going to press, Hachette Learning cannot be held responsible for the content of any website mentioned in this book. It is sometimes possible to find a relocated web page by typing in the address of the home page for a website in the URL window of your browser.

Hachette UK's policy is to use papers that are natural, renewable and recyclable products and made from wood grown in well-managed forests and other controlled sources. The logging and manufacturing processes are expected to conform to the environmental regulations of the country of origin.

To order, please visit www.HachetteLearning.com or contact Customer Service at education@hachette.co.uk / +44 (0)1235 827827.

ISBN: 9781036005184

First published in 2026 by Hachette Learning (a trading division of Hodder & Stoughton Limited),
An Hachette UK Company
Carmelite House
50 Victoria Embankment
London EC4Y 0DZ

www.HachetteLearning.com

The authorised representative in the EEA is Hachette Ireland, 8 Castlecourt Centre, Dublin 15, D15 XTP3, Ireland (email: info@hbgi.ie)

Impression number 10 9 8 7 6 5 4 3 2 1

Year 2030 2029 2028 2027 2026

Cover photo © GoodStudio- stock.adobe.com

Illustrations by Hyphen S.A./Konstantina Kyratzidou

Typeset by Hyphen S.A.

Printed and bound in Great Britain by Bell & Bain Ltd, Glasgow

A catalogue record for this title is available from the British Library.

FSC www.fsc.org MIX Paper | Supporting responsible forestry FSC™ C104740

Contents

How to use this book

Think about successful athletes. Athletes learn about their sport, and they practise and train hard to become excellent performers.

You can excel at communication by learning how to identify the purpose and audience for communicating and then training yourself to answer different types of questions.

You are going to work through **Practice paper 1** with your teacher. This will help you to:

- Read questions carefully and work out what type of answer to give.
- Learn how you can get good results even if your answer is different from everybody else's.
- Understand what the different ratings mean and see how you can improve your rating.
- Reflect on your own work to help you see what you did well and what you can improve in the next task.

Each task in this book has three supporting features.

Before you start …

This section helps you think carefully about questions and what it is you are being asked to do. There are different activities for each task.

Hints

These are given in the task itself to help you think about the questions and how you should answer them. As you progress, there will be fewer hints in the tasks.

Reflection

This section encourages you to think about your own learning and how you can improve on it.

Practice paper 1 also has a section called **How do you know how well you did?**

In this section, you can see how students answered the questions and what rating they were given. The aim of this section is to show you what you need to do to get the best possible results.

Practice paper 1

This task has two parts. For both parts, you must read **Source 1** and **Source 2**.

- Part 1 has questions 1 to 7.
- Part 2 has question 8.

→ Before you start ...

Look at these students' responses for the following task: As a Jamaican citizen, what does cultural heritage mean to you? Both students have the right answer, but Annika gets a better grade than Nadia. Can you see why?

Nadia's response	Annika's response
Cultural heritage is our identity and what makes us Jamaican. It is about our music like reggae.	Jamaican cultural heritage is a vibrant fusion of traditions from our historic past that reflects our resilience, our creativity and our passion for life. It is the heartbeat of our nation, the foundation upon which our identity is built. From the pulsating rhythm of reggae to the fiery cuisine of jerk chicken, our heritage is a symphony of experiences that captivates the soul. Jamaican cultural heritage is the glue that binds us together despite our differences.

Although both responses are correct, Nadia's response is limited.

Annika's response demonstrates a deep understanding of the prompt. It also has a clear and organised structure, evidence-based reasoning, original expression and expressive language. These qualities elevate the response to a higher level, demonstrating her ability to provide a descriptive and insightful definition of cultural heritage.

Look at the instruction words and phrases in the Knowledge boxes below. Which Knowledge box goes with Nadia's and Annika's responses?

Write **Recalling information**, **Skills and concepts**, **Strategic thinking** or **Extended thinking** next to their name below. Think about what each instruction means in the Knowledge boxes before you answer the question.

Nadia ______________________

Annika ______________________

Recalling information	Skills and concepts	Strategic thinking	Extended thinking
Remember, recall, recognise or locate basic details and ideas. There is one correct answer.	Explain, show relationships; use your skills and what you know to make decisions about what to do and how to do it. There is one correct answer.	Explain your thinking and give reasons for your answers. There are different answers and different ways to find the answers.	Plan, think and put ideas together to solve a problem. There are many possible answers and ways of solving the problem.

Look at the end of the test to check the Knowledge box that goes with Nadia's and Annika's responses.

Part 1

SOURCE 1

A Guide to Jamaica's History and Independence

A Journey Through Time

If you are going to visit Jamaica, you will be interested to learn a little about this beautiful country with a proud history. Jamaica's transformation into an independent nation is proof of resilience, cultural blending and staunch spirit. These factors are woven into the fabric of Jamaican history which makes it a proud nation.

Pre-Historic Jamaica: Revealing the Past

Jamaica's pre-historic era is covered in mystery. Archaeological excavations have revealed artifacts of settlements that date back to 4000 BC. The Arawak and the Taíno people are the island's earliest inhabitants who established distinct cultural identities.

The Arrival of European Colonisation

- First, the famous explorer, Christopher Columbus, set foot on Jamaican soil in 1494.
- Then in 1509, the island became a colony of Spain.
- The Spanish introduced their language, religion and agricultural practices, leaving a legacy on Jamaican culture.

The Transformation into a British Colony

After nearly 150 years of Spanish rule, the British seized control of the island from the Spanish. Their colonial rule lasted over 300 years. The British brought their own customs, laws and social structures, further shaping Jamaica's cultural tapestry.

The Road to Independence: Achieving Self-governance

Self-governance was achieved through the determination of many Jamaicans. National heroes, such as Paul Bogle and George William Gordon, resisted the laws of the British. In 1962, Jamaica finally achieved independence from British rule. Their sovereignty was marked by nationwide celebrations that brought a sense of pride.

A Symbol of Independence

Amidst the jubilation of Independence Day, the symbol of the nation's autonomy with its distinct pattern of a yellow cross and the colours of green and black was raised for the first time. Today, Jamaica stands as a vibrant and independent nation, embracing its unique identity which is evidence of its resilience. Its rich history, cultural diversity and warm hospitality continue to captivate visitors from around the world.

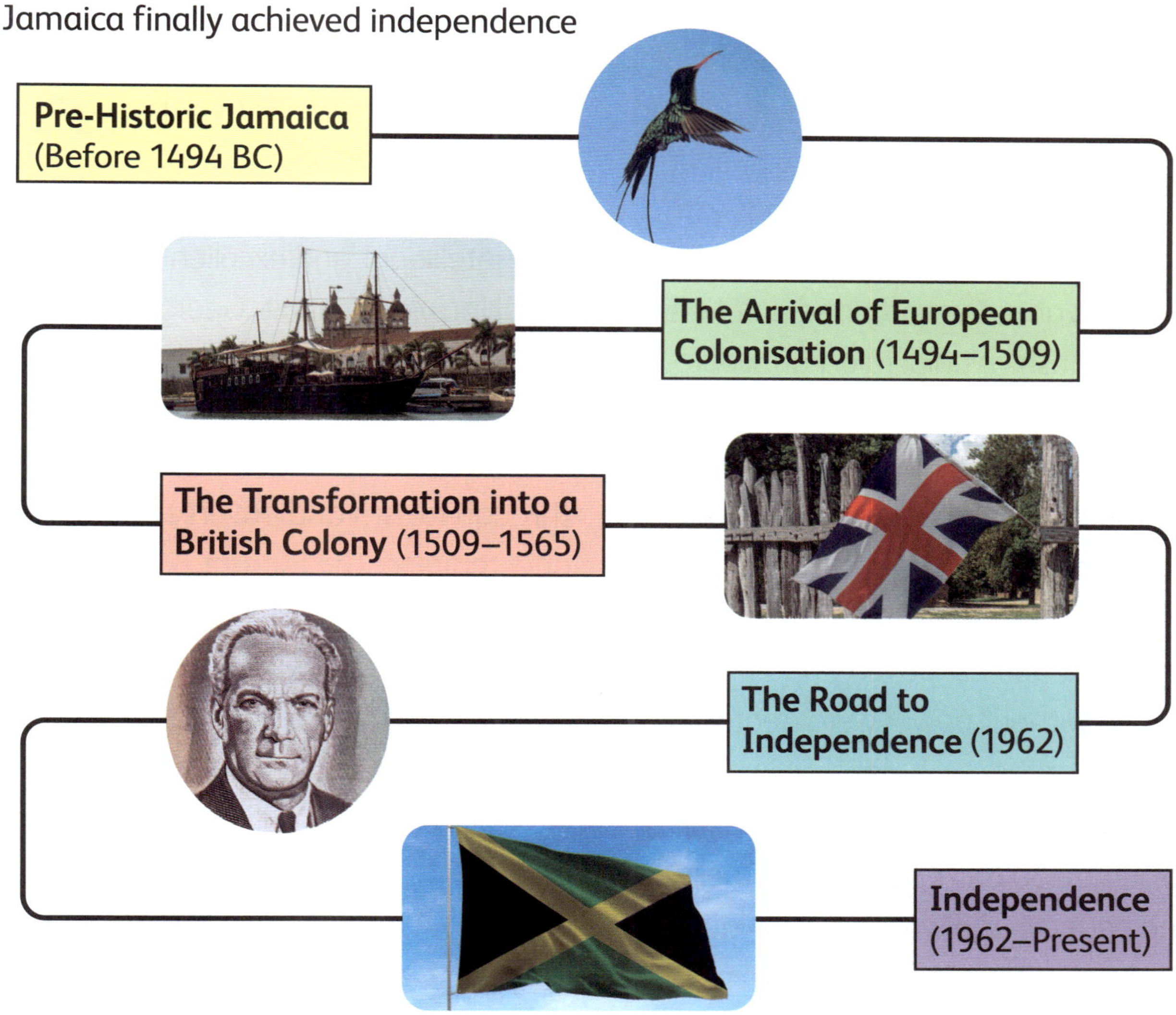

SOURCE 2

Two National Heroes

Paul Bogle

(1822–24 October 1865)

Paul Bogle is one of the seven National Heroes of Jamaica. He was born near Morant Bay, St Thomas in 1822. Although slavery had not yet been abolished, he was born free and owned a plot of land in the farming community. There were very few people from the area who were allowed to vote (around a hundred), but he was one of them. He was very interested in politics as a way to address the inequalities in society. He became good friends with George William Gordon, who shared his concerns about poverty and unfairness under British colonial rule. Paul Bogle was also very religious and became a Deacon of the Native Baptist Church in Stony Gut, where he helped educate the church congregation. In 1865, Bogle led a march to Morant Bay Courthouse to protest against poverty and the way people without power were treated by those in authority. It became known as the Morant Bay Rebellion. Bogle is remembered for fighting for fairness and equality and was made a National Hero a long time after his death in 1969.

George William Gordon

(1820–23 October 1865)

George William Gordon is another of the seven National Heroes of Jamaica. Born in 1820, his mother was enslaved and his father was a planter from Scotland. George William Gordon was not educated at school, but he taught himself to read and write. At ten years old, he went to live with his godfather who ran his own business in Black River. He learned a lot from his godfather's work and grew up to be a businessman. He was very intelligent and excellent at public speaking. As an adult, George William Gordon attended Paul Bogle's Church and shared many of same views on the unfairness of colonial society seen through racism and poverty. He was arrested after the Morant Bay Rebellion in 1865 even though there was no evidence that he was involved. He was not given a fair trial but was sentenced to death by British colonial authorities. He was also made a National Hero in 1969.

Question 1

a Go back to **Source 1** and become a text detective! Match each text feature (**i** to **iv**) with the meaning (**a** to **d**) that best describes it.

	Text feature
i	Headings
ii	Bullet points
iii	Subheadings
iv	Graphics

	Meaning
a	These provide more specific information about the main topic of the heading.
b	These can include images, charts or graphs.
c	These list important details in a concise way.
d	These can present information in a clear and organised way.

b Write an example of each text feature in the table. One has been done for you.

	Text feature	An example from Source 1
i	Headings	
ii	Bullet points	
iii	Subheadings	
iv	Graphics	*Timeline*

Skim the text quickly to see how it is organised. Then, scan and read the text more carefully to find the detail that you need.

Question 2

a Which headings from **Source 1** would you look at to find out about Jamaica before independence?

____

____

b What do we call the sentence that introduces the main point of the text? Circle the correct answer.

i concluding sentence
ii transition sentence
iii topic sentence
iv supporting sentence

Question 3

Summarise the most important information from **Source 1**.

Question 4

Who is the intended audience of **Source 1**? Use evidence from the text to support your answer.

Question 5

Which aspect of the **Source 1** text do you find most interesting? Describe what you would like to find out more about and the different ways you would do your research.

Question 6

If you were writing your own version of the **Source 1** text, would you include the same information? What would you do differently?

Question 7

Use all the sources to help you answer these questions.

a What is the earliest date mentioned across all sources?

b Which country ruled Jamaica when Paul Bogle was alive?

c Find one piece of evidence from **Source 1** and one piece of evidence from **Source 2** that demonstrates Jamaica's resilience against colonialism.

Source 1 evidence

Source 2 evidence

Part 2

Question 8

Your parents' friend, Mrs Brown, is 80 years old and remembers what Jamaica was like before independence.

Write a letter telling Mrs Brown that you are doing a school project on Jamaica's road to independence. Briefly write what you learned about Paul Bogle and George William Gordon in the Jamaican independence movement. Ask what it was like to live in Jamaica before independence and how times have changed.

- **Paragraph 1:** Introduce yourself. Explain briefly why you are writing.
- **Paragraph 2:** Describe what you have already learned.
- **Paragraph 3:** Politely ask for the information you want to find out.
- **Paragraph 4:** Thank Mrs Brown for her time and consideration. Tell her that you look forward to hearing from her.

Remember to add your address and the date in the top right-hand corner.

Dear Mrs Brown,

I hope this letter finds you well. My name is ____________________

and my parents are good friends of yours. I am writing to you because

____

____.

We have been studying the Jamaican independence movement at school.

It has been really interesting and I have learned ______________________

____

____

____.

I would love to know more about what it was like before Jamaica became independent.

I would be very grateful if you could ______________________

____

____

____.

Thank you for reading my letter and ______________________

____

____

____.

Yours sincerely,

____

ICT and Social Studies link: Create a digital timeline using tools like Canva or PowerPoint to present key events in the lives of Paul Bogle and George William Gordon.

Practice paper 1 Self-evaluation

How do you know how well you did?

Here is the Knowledge box that goes with Nadia and Annika's responses:

Nadia: Recalling
Nadia's response recalls basic information.

Annika: Skills and concepts
Annika's response puts ideas together and suggests how to solve a problem, which is extending thinking.

Part 1

Now that you have worked through Part 1 of Practice paper 1, you are going to look at some answers that students gave to see how they were rated. Then you can rate your own answers using this scale.

Remember: There are often many ways to show understanding. Your response doesn't have to look exactly like the examples to be valid.

1 Beginning	2 Developing	3 Proficient	4 Highly proficient
Answers show limited understanding of the concept. The student may need more support, practice or clarification to develop their ideas further.	Answers shows some evidence that the student partly understands the concepts.	Answers show that the student is competent and understands most of the concepts.	Answers show that the student understands all the concepts very well and may have found the task quite easy.

Different thinkers may reach proficiency in different ways – by writing, drawing, speaking or explaining in their own words.

We will look at answers to the four different levels of questions.

Question 1

a Match the text features **i** to **iv** with their meanings **a** to **d**.

	Text feature
i	Headings
ii	Bullet points
iii	Subheadings
iv	Graphics

	Meaning
d	These can present information in a clear and organised way.
c	These list important details in a concise way.
a	These provide more specific information about the main topic of the heading.
b	These can include images, charts or graphs.

b Write an example of each text feature in the table.

	Text feature	An example from Source 1
i	Headings	A Journey Through Time
ii	Bullet points	First, the famous explorer, Christopher Columbus, set foot on Jamaican soil in 1494.
iii	Subheadings	Revealing the Past
iv	Graphics	Timeline

1 Beginning / Word recognition and fluency: Apply word recognition strategies found most helpful before, during and after reading.

Tasks a and b are examples of the skills of recall and reproduction. The tasks require students to simply match text features with their corresponding meanings in Question 1a, and identify and recall information from the text for Question 1b. There is no need for critical thinking, analysis or application of knowledge.

Question 2

a Which headings from **Source 1** would you look at to find out about Jamaica before independence?

The headings "Pre-Historic Jamaica: Revealing the Past" and "The Arrival of European Colonisation" would indicate that these sections of the text will discuss Jamaica's history before the time of independence from British rule.

2 Developing / Research and Study Skills: Use table of contents and index to locate information in texts. Use graphs, maps and charts.

This task asks to locate information about a particular period and, therefore, requires the ability to identify and extract specific information from a text. The text provides a clear chronological overview of Jamaica's history, with each heading marking a distinct period.

b What do we call the sentence that introduces the main point of the text?

i concluding sentence
ii transition sentence
(iii) topic sentence
iv supporting sentence

2 Developing / Word Recognition and Fluency: Identify and reflect on (or use) word recognition strategies found most helpful before, during and after reading.

The task requires the student to recall and apply basic knowledge and identify and define different types of sentences, including topic sentences.

Question 3

Summarise the most important information from **Source 1**.

Jamaica has a rich and complex history that dates back to 4000 BC. The island was first inhabited by the Arawak and the Taino people who were later enslaved by Spanish settlers. The British took control of Jamaica in the 17th century and ruled for over three hundred years. In 1962, Jamaica finally gained its independence from Britain. Today, Jamaica is a vibrant and independent nation with a unique culture and history.

3 Proficient / Comprehension: Summarise main findings in a text.

The task requires the student to apply the information from the text to a new situation. To identify the most important points, students need to make judgements about what is important, organise the information in a logical order and use their own words to express the information.

Question 4

Who is the intended audience of **Source 1**? Use evidence from the text to support your answer.

The text begins by stating that it is a guide to Jamaica's history. This suggests that the text is intended to provide information to a general audience, such as tourists who are not familiar with the subject and are interested in learning about Jamaica's history.

2 Developing / Comprehension: Skim, scan and apply other reading strategies to locate main ideas and other specific information in text.

The task asks the reader to interpret the text to determine who the intended audience is, which is supported by evidence in the text.

Question 5

Which aspect of the **Source 1** text do you find most interesting? Describe what you would like to find out more about and the different ways you would do your research.

Comprehension: Self-select reading materials and share their reading interests.	
The most interesting aspect of the text is the transformation of Jamaica into an independent nation. This reflects the country's resilience and strong spirit. I would like to find out more about the struggles and achievements of the Jamaican people during their fight for independence.	I found the aspect of the text that describes how Jamaica's culture has been shaped by its long history of colonisation to be the most interesting. I would like to learn more about the different cultures that have come to Jamaica and how they have influenced the island's music, cuisine and traditions. I would research this topic by reading books and articles about Jamaican history and culture, visiting museums and historical sites in Jamaica and talking to Jamaican people.
1 Beginning *Beginning: The student recalls information from the text. The student identifies the most interesting aspect of the text and expresses their desire to learn more about it, but they do not state how they would do further research.*	3 Proficient *This response accurately summarises the main points of the text and shows understanding of the relationships between the ideas. Additionally, the response expresses personal interest in the topic and indicates a willingness to engage in further research.*

Question 6

If you were writing your own version of the **Source 1** text, would you include the same information? What would you do differently?

Comprehension: Identify and discuss connections with texts: text-to-self, text-to-text and text-to-world; interpret texts accurately and with expression.	
I would include the same information in my own version of this text, but I would present it in a less serious manner, using storytelling techniques. I would also focus more on the arrival of Columbus, the struggle for independence and the sense of Jamaican pride after gaining independence.	I would go beyond simply recounting events and delve into the deeper historical context, analysing the motivations, perspectives and consequences of these historical occurrences. I would also explore the intangible aspects of Jamaican history, such as the cultural blending, resilience and staunch spirit that have shaped the nation's identity.

② Developing	④ Highly proficient
This response, as it is, involves factual recall and basic comprehension. The response is simple and straightforward, using clear language and avoiding complex vocabulary or sentence structures. Developing responses provide a summary of events and concepts, without delving into deeper analysis or interpretation.	*This response shows critical analysis and synthesis. The response is written in a sophisticated manner, using more complex vocabulary and sentence structures. It proposes engagement in deeper analysis of historical events and concepts, examining their causes, consequences and wider implications.*

Question 7

Use all the sources to help you answer these questions.

a What is the earliest date mentioned across all sources? 4000 BC

b Which country ruled Jamaica when Paul Bogle was alive? The British

① Beginning / Comprehension: Skim, scan and apply other reading strategies to locate main ideas and other specific information in text.

The answers require the student to recall information that has been explicitly taught or presented to them.

c Find one piece of evidence from **Source 1** and one piece of evidence from **Source 2** that demonstrates Jamaica's resilience against colonialism.

Source 1 evidence

Source 1 states that Jamaica's change into an independent nation was "proof of resilience, cultural blending and staunch spirit". This demonstrates that Jamaicans were able to resist colonialism and achieve independence, which is evidence of resilience.

Source 2 evidence

Source 2 states that Paul Bogle and George William Gordon were national heroes who resisted the laws of the British. This demonstrates that Jamaicans were not afraid to fight for their freedom, which is also evidence of resilience.

③ Proficient / Comprehension: Skim, scan and apply other reading strategies to locate main ideas and other specific information in text.

The answer requires the student to analyse and synthesise information from two different sources to support a claim. This level of analysis requires more critical thinking and reasoning than a beginning answer which would simply require the student to recall information from one source.

Part 2

Question 8

Your parents' friend, Mrs Brown, is 80 years old and remembers what it was like to live before Jamaica gained independence.

Write a letter telling Mrs Brown that you are doing a school project on Jamaica's road to independence. Briefly write what you learned about Paul Bogle and George William Gordon in the Jamaican independence movement. Ask what it was like to live in Jamaica before independence and how times have changed.

- **Paragraph 1:** Introduce yourself. Explain briefly why you are writing.
- **Paragraph 2:** Describe what you have already learned.
- **Paragraph 3:** Politely ask for the information you want to find out.
- **Paragraph 4**: Thank Mrs Brown for her time and consideration. Tell her that you look forward to hearing from her.

Suggested response:

[Your address and date]

Dear Mrs Brown,

I hope this letter finds you well. My name is ____________________ and my parents are good friends of yours. I am writing to you because I am doing a school project about Jamaica's road to independence. I was wondering if you could tell me what it was like to live through the time of colonisation and how Jamaica has changed after gaining independence. I am interested in learning more about the lives of Paul Bogle and George William Gordon.

We have been studying the Jamaican independence movement at school. It has been really interesting and I have learned that Paul Bogle was a Baptist deacon in Stony Gut, St Thomas, Jamaica. He was a leader of the Morant Bay Rebellion of 1865, which was against the British colonial rule. George William Gordon was a member of the Jamaican Assembly and a strong supporter for justice for Jamaicans. In 1865, he was arrested in connection with the Morant Bay Rebellion.

I would love to know more about what it was like before Jamaica became independent. I would be very grateful if you could tell me what the challenges and opportunities were that people faced. What changes have taken place in Jamaica since independence? I am interested in hearing your personal experiences. Your perspective would be invaluable to me as I learn more about Jamaica's history.

Thank you for reading my letter and I look forward to hearing from you soon.

Yours sincerely,

[Your name]

Reflection

Use your answers to the task to assess your own learning.

- List the question numbers.
- Rate your work on each question using this scale:

Question	Below standard	On track	Above standard

Practice paper 2

This task has two parts. For both parts, you must read **Source 1** and **Source 2**.

- Part 1 has questions 1 to 6.
- Part 2 has question 7.

→ Before you start ...

Look at these students' responses for the following task: Why are national heroes honoured by Jamaicans? Both students have the right answer, but Annika gets a better grade than Nadia. Can you see why?

Nadia's response	Annika's response
Jamaica honours national heroes like Nanny of the Maroons to celebrate their contributions to Jamaica's development.	By commemorating the national hero Nanny through art and environmental awareness, Jamaica aims to celebrate her legacy as both a freedom fighter and protector of nature, promoting national pride, empowering women and fostering a vision of greatness for the future.

Although both responses are correct, Nadia's response states a general fact about Jamaica honouring its national heroes. It does not require any deep analysis or interpretation.

Annika's response goes beyond simply stating a fact. It analyses the purpose of commemorating Nanny. It identifies objectives, such as promoting national pride, empowering women and fostering environmental awareness. It requires understanding the historical context and significance of Nanny's legacy.

Look at the instruction words and phrases in the Knowledge boxes below. Which Knowledge box goes with Nadia's and Annika's responses?

Write **Recalling information**, **Skills and concepts**, **Strategic thinking** or **Extended thinking** next to their name below. Think about what each instruction means in the Knowledge boxes before you answer the question.

Nadia ______________________________

Annika ______________________________

Recalling information	Skills and concepts	Strategic thinking	Extended thinking
Remember, recall, recognise or locate basic details and ideas. There is one correct answer.	Explain, show relationships; use your skills and what you know to make decisions about what to do and how to do it. There is one correct answer.	Explain your thinking and give reasons for your answers. There are different answers and different ways to find the answers.	Plan, think and put ideas together to solve a problem. There are many possible answers and ways of solving the problem.

Part 1

ICT and Social Studies link: You could use Google Slides or Canva to create your own image of Nanny of the Maroons.

SOURCE 1

Nanny Reimagined as Protector of the Natural Environment

On 27 November 2022, the Natural History Division of the Institute of Jamaica (IOJ) in Kingston launched an exciting art exhibition inspired by the Jamaican national hero, Nanny of the Maroons, called "Reimagining Nanny". All of the artworks exhibited were created to teach visitors about Jamaica's old traditions and to imagine Nanny as a guardian of nature in the Blue Mountains. Pictures and paintings were created by talented artists, such as Richard Natto, Ibaya Art, Lisa Callender and Segun Bamidele Aiyesan. The exhibition was put together by people from the Institute of Jamaica together with partner organisations: New York University (NYU) and the Jamaica Conservation and Development Trust (JCDT).

SOURCE 2

Honouring Queen Nanny

Minister Olivia Grange lauded the Institute of Jamaica (IOJ) for promoting Jamaica's natural heritage. In a speech delivered on her behalf by Permanent Secretary in the Ministry, Denzil Thorpe, Queen Nanny's positive impact on the environment was highlighted and her role in inspiring Jamaican women.

Minister Grange expressed a vision for Jamaicans to excel in all aspects of life, using Queen Nanny as a role model. The art exhibition was just one of many events to celebrate 60 years of Jamaican independence under the theme "Jamaica 60 – Reigniting a Nation for Greatness".

The question word at the beginning of each question is called an interrogative pronoun. There are **five** interrogative pronouns.

Question 1

Complete the questions with the correct interrogative pronoun.

a ______________________ owns that red car?

b ______________________ time is the movie starting?

c ______________________ restaurant is the best in town?

d ______________________ is this smartphone?

e ______________________ did you go on vacation last year?

Question 2

Write a question beginning with each of the interrogative pronouns in **a** to **d**. For example, "What is that smell?"

a What …?

____

b Who …?

____

c Which …?

d Whose …?

Question 3

Use **Sources 1** and **2** to answer these questions.

a What is the theme of the art exhibition?

b Who was commissioned to create the art pieces?

c Which word best describes the meaning of "lauded" in **Source 2**? Circle the correct answer.

i condemned

ii criticised

iii mentioned

iv praised

Question 4

a Which word best describes the meaning of "highlighted" in **Source 2**? Circle the correct answer.

i picked out

ii emphasised

iii represented

iv promoted

b What did Minister Olivia Grange say about the national hero Nanny?

____

____

Question 5

Look at the table below and the example of the question word **what** in the past, present and future tense. Identify which question from **a** to **i** is written in the past, the present and the future tense and write the letter in the correct space in the table.

a Who organised the art exhibition in 2022?

b Which division of the IOJ organised the project?

c Whose message was read by Permanent Secretary in the Ministry, Denzil Thorpe?

d Whose vision is for Jamaicans to excel in all aspects of their lives?

e Which partner organisations collaborated with the IOJ in organising the project?

f Who commissions the collection of works in 2022?

g Who will commission the collection of works in 2022?

h Who had a positive impact on the environment and inspired Jamaican women?

If the verb ends in -ed, it is past tense. For example, **commissioned**.

Interrogative question word	Past	Present	Future
What	What were the five art pieces that were unveiled on 27 November 2022?	What are the five art pieces that were unveiled?	What will the five art pieces at the IOJ be?
Who	____________ ____________	____________ ____________	____________ ____________
Which	____________ ____________	____________ ____________	____________ ____________
Whose	____________ ____________	____________ ____________	____________ ____________

Question 6

a Based only on the sentences below, which two options indicate that the exhibition was created to promote culture and history? Circle the answers.

i A collection of five art pieces under the theme "Reimagining Nanny" was unveiled on 27 November 2022.

ii The collection of works was commissioned in 2022 to raise awareness of Jamaica's historical customs.

iii The project was organised by the IOJ in collaboration with the JCDT and NYU to increase the knowledge of the ancient customs and traditions of the Caribbean.

b Read the statement and use it to answer the question: Which two points from the exhibition and the Minister's message support this statement? Circle the answers.

> "... a vision for Jamaicans to excel in all aspects of life, using Queen Nanny as a role model."

i Queen Nanny continues to motivate young Jamaican girls to be the best version of themselves.

ii The exhibition highlighted the untold stories about Nanny who was a great Jamaican woman.

iii The Minister said that Jamaicans should strive to be like Nanny and excel in all areas of life.

iv The Minister praised the IOJ for promoting Jamaica's natural heritage and environment.

Part 2

Question 7

Based on the information in both sources, you will plan and then write an essay on how the exhibition "Reimagining Nanny" contributes to promoting Jamaica's national identity and heritage.

a Create a mind map that you will use for your essay. Organise your information by noting facts and other points of interest form **Sources 1** and **2**.

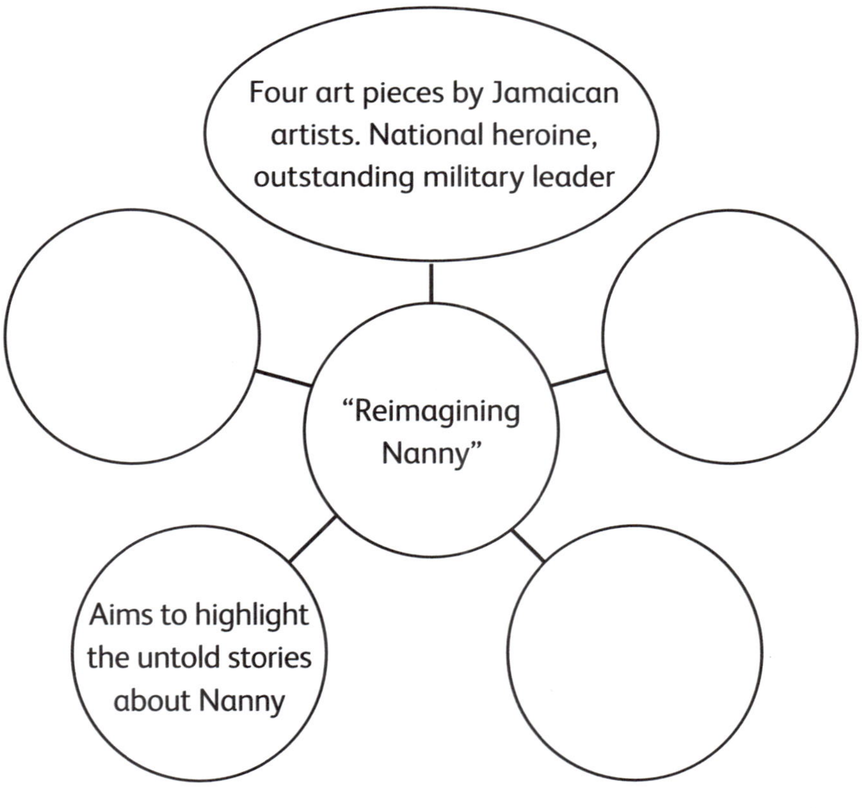

Have an introduction, a main body and a conclusion.
Give details from the two sources in your own words.

b In your essay:
Explain how the exhibition shows Nanny of the Maroons as a symbol of Jamaican strength, resilience and cultural significance.

Provide examples from the Minister's message to support your comments. Your response should demonstrate an understanding of the connection between art, culture and national identity.

Reflection

Use your answers to the task to analyse your strengths and weaknesses.

- What areas are you good at?

- Which areas require more work?

- What work will you do?

Practice paper 3

This task has two parts. For both parts, you must read **Source 1** and **Source 2**.

- Part 1 has questions 1 to 6.
- Part 2 has question 7.

→ Before you start …

Look at these students' responses for the following task: Why are the Blue Mountains important to Jamaica? Both students have the right answer, but Annika gets a better grade than Nadia. Can you see why?

Nadia's response	Annika's response
The Blue Mountains are important to Jamaica because they are the highest mountains on the island and offer beautiful views.	The Blue Mountains hold immense significance for Jamaica, not only for their breathtaking landscapes and diverse ecosystems, but also as a historical refuge for the Maroons and a testament to the island's unique cultural heritage, earning them well-deserved protection as a UNESCO World Heritage Site.

Although both responses are correct, Nadia's response is limited and focuses on a basic detail which is an observable fact.

Annika's response delves deeper and presents a more insightful perspective on the importance of the Blue Mountains.

Look at the instruction words and phrases in the Knowledge boxes below. Which Knowledge box goes with Nadia and Annika's responses?

Write **Recalling information**, **Skills and concepts**, **Strategic thinking** or **Extended thinking** next to their name below. Think about what each instruction means in the Knowledge boxes before you answer the question.

Nadia ______________________

Annika ______________________

Recalling information	Skills and concepts	Strategic thinking	Extended thinking
Remember, recall, recognise or locate basic details and ideas. There is one correct answer.	Explain, show relationships; use your skills and what you know to make decisions about what to do and how to do it. There is one correct answer.	Explain your thinking and give reasons for your answers. There are different answers and different ways to find the answers.	Plan, think and put ideas together to solve a problem. There are many possible answers and ways of solving the problem.

Part 1

SOURCE 1

Discover Jamaica

1 Beyond the Beat in Jamaica: A Land of **Enthralling** Landscapes

Jamaica's attraction goes beyond friendly people and reggae rhythms. Nature lovers who explore beyond the usual spots will discover amazing **geological wonders**.

6 Majestic Mountains and Sculptural Plateaus

Jamaica's mountains were formed long ago by volcanoes. The Blue Mountains in the east rise steeply and are exciting to climb. To the north, the John Crow Mountains are made of soft limestone. Rain and water slowly wear away the limestone, creating amazing shapes called "Karst formations". These are some of the most unique landforms in the world.

14 Hidden Waters and Intriguing Caves

Most rivers in Jamaica are still a mystery. But for the **intrepid** explorer, they hide special surprises including waterfalls and caves that tell stories from the island's past.

[19] Coastal Contrasts

Jamaica's coastline has many kinds of beauty. The **rugged** north was shaped by **relentless** waves and wind. In the west, soft beaches and calm waves create peaceful views. The south has high cliffs that rise over the blue sea.

From tall mountains to quiet rivers, Jamaica's land is full of amazing places to explore. Whether you love hiking or swimming, there's something for you. So, put on your hiking boots, grab your swimsuit, and enjoy Jamaica's natural beauty.

SOURCE 2

The Blue and John Crow Mountains National Park

Often referred to as the "lungs of Jamaica," the breathtaking Blue and John Crow Mountains National Park stands as Jamaica's sole national park and, wow, is it something special! This haven of rainforest serves as a sanctuary for wildlife, boasting an impressive array of over eight hundred plant species, two hundred types of birds and the majestic giant swallowtail, the largest butterfly in the western hemisphere. With its cascading waterfalls and lush landscapes, this Jamaican gem is also famous for nurturing the world-renowned Jamaican Blue Mountain coffee. But wait, there is more to this paradise than meets the eye. The Blue and John Crow Mountains hold a significant place in Jamaica's history. They served as a refuge for the Maroons who sought shelter from their captors and established settlements in these mountains, using them as a base for their fight for freedom. Recognising its importance, the park was designated a UNESCO World Heritage Site in 2015. Only an hour's drive from Kingston, this park is easily accessible and definitely worth a trip. Visitors can immerse themselves in the beauty of the terrain through hiking and exploration.

For those seeking a luxurious experience, Strawberry Hill, the hotel where Bob Marley once stayed in the 1970s, offers accommodation amidst the stunning surroundings.

Question 1

Re-read **Source 1** and circle the correct answers.

a The word "enthralling" in line 1 is closest in meaning to:

i pleasant

ii entertaining

iii fascinating

iv enjoyable

b The words "geological wonders" in line 5 are closest in meaning to:

i cultural paradise

ii physical paradise

iii tropical paradise

iv unexplored paradise

c The word "intrepid" in line 16 is closest in meaning to:

i frightened

ii fearless

iii cautious

iv careful

d The word "rugged" in line 21 is closest in meaning to:

i rocky

ii smooth

iii cool

iv stormy

e The word "relentless" in line 21 is closest in meaning to:

i occasional

ii irregular

iii continuous

iv gentle

Question 2

Read **Source 1** and complete the blank boxes on the map with the words below.

1 Summit	2 Base	3 Gradient	4 Limestone

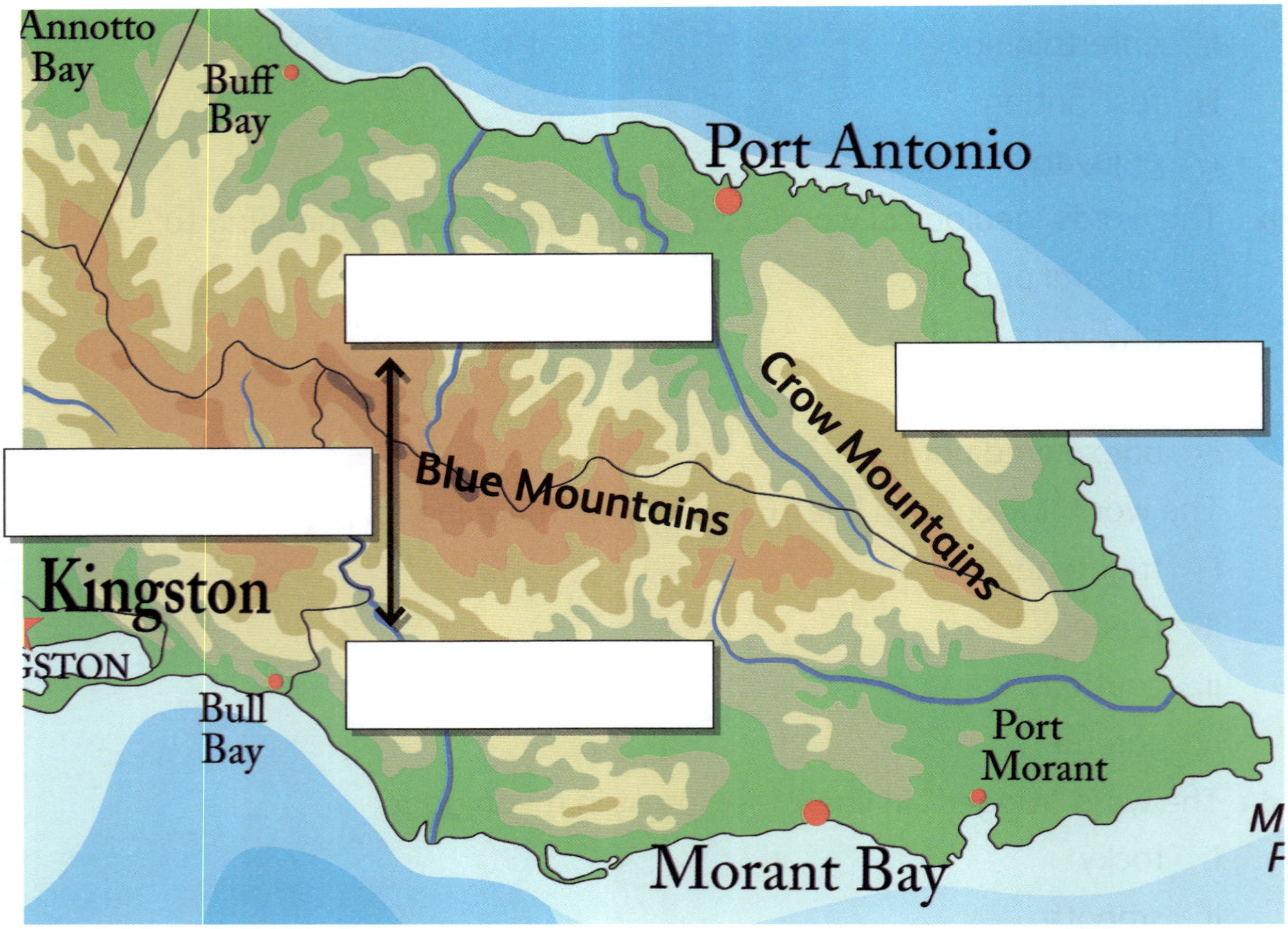

Question 3

What is the purpose of the **Source 1** text? Circle the answer.

i to entertain

ii to distract

iii to persuade

iv to express feelings

Question 4

Identify five words or phrases in the **Source 1** text that indicate whether the author has a positive or negative viewpoint.

	Example	Positive or negative?
1		
2		
3		
4		
5		

Adjectives modify or describe details about a noun. They often give an indication of the speaker's or writer's viewpoint. Look at these words. The two adjectives are highlighted in bold: **vibrant** people, **heart-pounding** climb.

Question 5

Complete the table below with the adjectives from the box. An example of each has been done for you.

magnificent disappointing distinctive substandard splendid gorgeous unsatisfactory bad fine acceptable wonderful suitable

Viewpoint	Words
Positive	*magnificent*
Negative	*disappointing*
Neutral / Factual	*distinctive*

Question 6

Refer to both **Sources 1** and **2** to answer these questions. Both sources describe Jamaica's natural beauty.

ICT and Geography Link: You could use Google Earth or an interactive map tool to explore the Blue and John Crow Mountains. Pin landmarks and add captions using key geographical terms.

a How do both sources describe this beauty in a similar way?

____

____

____

____

b How are the ways they describe this beauty different?

____

____

____

____

Use your own words to refer to specific examples from both texts to support your answer. The first one has been done as an example:

Both sources use positive adjectives to describe the area, such as **enthralling** in **Source 1** and **breathtaking** in **Source 2**.

c What is the main focus of each source and how can you tell?

Source 1: ______________________________

____

____

____

Source 2: ______________________________

____

____

____

d What kinds of activities and attractions do both sources mention for enjoying Jamaica's natural beauty?

e Is there an activity mentioned in one source that the other source does NOT mention?

f Compare both sources. How does the language used make you feel about visiting Jamaica's natural landscapes?

g Who do you think is the audience for each source? Give reasons for your answer.

____

____

____

____

Part 2

In your response, provide examples from the sources to support your arguments. Your response should demonstrate an understanding of the similarities and differences between the sources.

Question 7

Write an essay which includes an introduction, a main body and a conclusion on the following task:

Imagine you are planning a trip to the Blue and John Crow Mountains National Park. Which source would be more helpful in deciding where to go and what to do? Explain why.

Remember to include the following:

Introduction:

- Briefly engage the reader by mentioning your excitement about planning a trip to the Blue and John Crow Mountains National Park.
- Main Statement: Clearly state which source (**Source 1** or **2**) would be more helpful and why.

Main Body:

- Topic Sentence: Start each paragraph with a clear topic sentence, focusing on specific features in each source and how they relate to your decision-making.

Conclusion:

- Reaffirm your main statement: Briefly remind the reader why you prefer one source for planning your trip.
- Conclude with excitement: Express your anticipation for exploring the park based on the chosen source's guidance.

Reflection

Complete this flow chart.

My strengths

Evidence of my strengths

My goals for the next performance tasks

My plan to reach the goals

Practice paper 4

This task has two parts. For both parts, you must read **Source 1** and **Source 2**.

- Part 1 has questions 1 to 6.
- Part 2 has question 7.

→ Before you start …

Look at these students' responses for the following task: Why is poetry important? Both students have the right answer, but Annika gets a better grade than Nadia. Can you see why?

Nadia's response	Annika's response
Poetry is important in education because it teaches us about rhyming and life in an imaginative way.	*Poetry unveils hidden truths, condensing emotions like sunlight through a lens. It challenges perspectives, sparking empathy and growth, leaving us forever changed.*

Although both responses are correct, Nadia's response is a literal basic description.

Annika's response demonstrates a more in depth understanding and gives reasons for her answers.

Look at the instruction words and phrases in the Knowledge boxes below. Which Knowledge box goes with Nadia's and Annika's responses?

Write **Recalling information**, **Skills and concepts**, **Strategic thinking** or **Extended thinking** next to their name below. Think about what each instruction means in the Knowledge boxes before you answer the question.

Nadia ____________________ **Annika** ____________________

Recalling information	Skills and concepts	Strategic thinking	Extended thinking
Remember, recall, recognise or locate basic details and ideas. There is one correct answer.	Explain, show relationships; use your skills and what you know to make decisions about what to do and how to do it. There is one correct answer.	Explain your thinking and give reasons for your answers. There are different answers and different ways to find the answers.	Plan, think and put ideas together to solve a problem. There are many possible answers and ways of solving the problem.

Part 1

SOURCE 1

Valerie Bloom

Valerie was born and grew up in Jamaica and is a very successful writer, having published lots of wonderful stories and poems. She speaks English and Jamaican Creole and switches between them depending on who she is with. Nowadays she lives in the UK, so she mostly speaks in English, but she continues to write in both languages. If her stories are about Jamaica or Jamaican people, she uses a mix of both – she once said, "I just give a flavour of the language" – so that as many readers as possible can understand. When she writes poems, she lets the content help her decide the language. While some poems lend themselves to either English or Jamaican Creole, in an online interview, Valerie described how sometimes a poem will only flow in one of the languages. She explained this by saying, "the poem decides which language it wants to be written in".

SOURCE 2 Rain

She makes the trees sway with delight
She tells the long grass, "Shiver"
She puts the laughter in the stream
And the gurgle in the river

She drives the thunder grumbling off
Orders the wind to sing
Snuffs the lightning's fire out
Takes the roof tap-dancing

She pours a drink for the thirsty Earth
Washes the face of the sky
Puts a sparkle on the leaves
And a glint in the ocean's eye

She plays a tattoo on the windowpanes
Paints doors a darker brown
And creates a brand-new swimming pool
In the centre of the town

In anger, she will pound the ground
With the force of a cannonball
But happy, she sings a lullaby
This celestial waterfall

By Valerie Bloom

A proper noun is a type of noun that refers to a specific person, place or thing by its name.

ICT link: You could use a digital poetry tool like Book Creator or Google Slides to create and illustrate your own weather poem, inspired by Valerie Bloom's Rain.

Question 1

Identify the first five proper nouns in **Source 1**.

i ______

ii ______

iii ______

iv ______

v ______

Question 2

a How does living in Britain affect Valerie's language use?

______

______

b Valerie uses only the Jamaican language when she writes a novel about Jamaica or Jamaicans or things Jamaican. Circle your answer.

i True

ii False

c What does Valerie mean by "I just give a flavour of the language" when writing novels?

______

______

______

______

d What do you think Valerie means when she says, "the poem decides which language it wants to be written in"?

____

____

____

____

Question 3

Read **Source 2** and circle one answer for the following questions:

a What does the rain do to the trees?

- i It makes them bend over.
- ii It makes them dance and sway happily.
- iii It makes them shiver and cry.
- iv It makes them grow taller and stronger.

b What sound does the rain make the stream and river produce?

- i roar and crash
- ii gurgle and laugh
- iii whisper and sigh
- iv splash and bubble

c How does the rain control the weather?

- i She brings the Sun and warmth.
- ii She makes the clouds disappear.
- iii She chases away the thunder.
- iv She brings rainbows and butterflies.

d What does the rain do for the Earth and sky?

- i She makes them fight and argue.
- ii She refreshes the Earth and cleans the sky.
- iii She hides them from the Sun.
- iv She covers them in mud and dirt.

e How does the rain show its different moods?

i She is always gentle and quiet.

ii She changes her colours and shapes.

iii She sings loud and soft songs.

iv She can be both angry and peaceful.

Personification is a type of figurative language that applies human qualities to objects, animals or abstract ideas.

Question 4

Identify personification by writing three things where the rain does things that only a person can do. For example, in line 2, she **tells** the long grass to "shiver".

Question 5

Imagine you are caught outside in the rain. Using words from the poem, describe how you would feel and what you would see and hear.

Question 6

Do you think rain is a good thing or a bad thing? Explain your answer using evidence from the poem.

____

____

____

____

____

____

Part 2

Question 7

Write a poem of your own about rain, inspired by the imagery in *Rain* by Valerie Bloom.

- Choose a specific focus: Will your poem focus on a particular scene or feeling associated with rain? Do you want to capture its playful or powerful side?
- Use vivid imagery: Use descriptive language to create sensory details like sight, sound, smell and touch. Think about how rain transforms your surroundings.
- Personify the rain: Like Valerie Bloom, you can give the rain human qualities and actions. How does it interact with its environment? What emotions might it express?

Reflection

Complete these sentences.

- I found question ______________ easiest because

____

____

____

- I think question ______________ was challenging for me because

____

____

____

Practice paper 5

This task has two parts. For both parts, you must read **Source 1** and **Source 2**.

- Part 1 has questions 1 to 10.
- Part 2 has question 11.

→ Before you start ...

Look at these students' responses for the following task: Describe a sound that makes you happy. Both students have the right answer, but Annika gets a better grade than Nadia. Can you see why?

Nadia's response	Annika's response
My favourite sound is the happy giggle of a child. It makes me smile every time!	The emotional tone of a child's giggle is unparalleled. It embodies pure joy and innocence, reminding me of the beauty and simplicity of life. It is a sound that transcends language and culture, connecting us all on a fundamental level.

Although both responses are correct, Nadia's response is simple and direct, meeting the basic requirement of identifying a favourite sound and providing a basic reason.

Annika's response delves deeper, explaining the specific qualities of the sound, using richer vocabulary and figurative language to create a more descriptive and evocative experience for the reader.

Look at the instruction words and phrases in the Knowledge boxes below. Which Knowledge box goes with Nadia's and Annika's responses?

Write **Recalling information**, **Skills and concepts**, **Strategic thinking** or **Extended thinking** next to their name below. Think about what each instruction means in the Knowledge boxes before you answer the question.

Nadia ______________________

Annika ______________________

Recalling information	Skills and concepts	Strategic thinking	Extended thinking
Remember, recall, recognise or locate basic details and ideas. There is one correct answer.	Explain, show relationships; use your skills and what you know to make decisions about what to do and how to do it. There is one correct answer.	Explain your thinking and give reasons for your answers. There are different answers and different ways to find the answers.	Plan, think and put ideas together to solve a problem. There are many possible answers and ways of solving the problem.

Part 1

SOURCE 1

Visualisation

Vision

Sight allows humans to see the world around us. Light travels through the pupil of the eye and sends messages to the brain through the optic nerves. It is like a team working together to show us pictures! Some animals have super eyes that can see even when it is almost dark, like owls at night. But for humans, in total darkness, sight is impossible.

Reflection

When light waves meet a shiny surface like a mirror, they reverse back into your eyes, so you see your reflection.

Instruments of Science

Telescopes have powerful lenses to pick up distant light. Opposite to this is the microscope which uses the lens in reverse by drawing the light towards the eye, making an object appear larger than its size. Cameras capture light which passes through a lens and is focused onto electronic detectors.

ICT and Science link: You could use a digital animation tool (like Scratch or PowerPoint) to create a short visual explaining how sound travels to the brain or how refraction works.

Light passing through materials

Material that allows light to pass through it is called transparent, so the light does not reflect back. However, there are materials that allow some light through such as frosted glass or tracing paper which are called translucent. Translucent material allows some light to pass through, while simultaneously reflecting the rest.

Refraction is the redirection of a wave when the speed of light changes from one transparent material, such as air, to another, such as water, resulting in the light wave changing direction. If you put half of a pen in a bowl of water, it will appear bent due to refraction at the water surface.

SOURCE 2

Vibrations

[1]Sound travels through air as vibrations which we pick up through our eardrums. [2]When we hear something, the vibrations go into our ears, through some tiny bones and into a snail-shaped part in the inner ear called the cochlea. [3]Inside the cochlea, there are special cells that change the vibrations into electric signals. [4]These signals travel through a special wire (called the auditory nerve) to our brain. [5]After that, our brain listens to the signals and tells us what sound we heard – amazing, right? [6]A lot happens, but it happens very quickly! [7]Some sounds are nice, but some can be annoying. [8]Can you think of sounds that you do not like to hear? [9]Maybe it is your alarm clock in the morning or the piercing sound of a car alarm. [10]People sniffing is an annoying sound!

SOURCE 3

Sound or noise?

Can you hear those lovely sounds? Like the happy chirping of these crickets here on the ground or the gentle rustle of these leaves in this wind. Even the trickle of water in that fountain over there. Sounds can make us happy, but sometimes we wish our ears were not so sensitive! It is not nice when a door slams loudly or a dog barks fiercely. However, those loud sounds can be important, like when a fire alarm rings to warn us of danger. We should appreciate the wide variety of sounds around us, from the beautiful sound of birds singing to those that make us feel more tense, like car horns, breaking glass and people shouting. All these different sounds, whether we like them or not, contribute to the richness of our world.

Question 1

Before reading:

a look at the title of **Source 1**, *Visualisation*. What do you think the text will be about? What clues does the title give you?

____

____

b can you think of any questions you have about vision before reading the text?

____

____

Question 2

During reading:

a what does the **Source 1** text compare the human eye to? How does this comparison help you understand how vision works?

____

____

b what are some examples of animals with "super eyes" mentioned in the text? Why do you think these animals have special vision?

Question 3

After reading:

a explain the difference between transparent and translucent materials, using examples from **Source 1**.

b how does a telescope help us see distant objects? What is the opposite of how a telescope works?

c look at how the text demonstrates refraction by describing how a pen appears to bend if part of it is submerged in a bowl of water. Describe another example of refraction in your everyday life and explain why you think your example shows refraction in action. You can choose one of your own or use one of these:

- looking through a glass of water
- a straw in water
- a rainbow in the sky
- fish underwater.

Question 5

Critical thinking:

a Imagine you are designing a new instrument that uses light to help people see better. What would it look like and how would it work? What would it allow people to see?

____

____

____

____

b Why do you think it is important for us to learn about light and vision? How does this knowledge affect our lives?

____

____

____

____

Question 6

Read sentences 1 to 10 of the text from **Source 2** and write whether each sentence is a declarative, exclamatory or an interrogative sentence. The first one is done as an example.

- Declarative sentences state a fact or make a statement and usually end with a full stop (.).
- Exclamatory sentences express strong emotion, like surprise or excitement and often end with an exclamation mark (!).
- Interrogative sentences ask a question and end with a question mark (?).

1 Sound travels through air as vibrations which we pick up through our eardrums.

declarative

[2]When we hear something, the vibrations go into our ears, through some tiny bones and into a snail-shaped part in the inner ear called the cochlea.

---

[3]Inside the cochlea, there are special cells that change the vibrations into electric signals.

---

[4]These signals travel through a special wire (called the auditory nerve) to our brain.

---

[5]After that, our brain listens to the signals and tells us what sound we heard – amazing, right?

---

[6]A lot happens, but it happens very quickly!

---

[7]Some sounds are nice, but some can be annoying.

---

[8]Can you think of sounds that you do not like to hear?

---

[9]Maybe it is your alarm clock in the morning or the piercing sound of a car alarm.

---

[10]People sniffing is an annoying sound!

Question 7

For each demonstrative pronoun in the table below, identify whether the pronoun is singular or plural and whether it refers to something close or further away. Complete the table. One has been done for you.

S for Singular or **P** for plural.

N for Near or **F** for Far.

	Demonstrative pronoun	Singular or Plural	Near or Far
1	those	P	F
2	these		
3	that		
4	this		

Here is an example to help you:

Original sentence: Look at <u>that</u> beautiful tree over <u>there</u>!

Rewritten sentence: Look at <u>this</u> beautiful tree over <u>here</u>!

Question 8

Rewrite the following sentences/phrases from **Source 3** using a different demonstrative pronoun and change any other words that support the meaning of the sentence.

a Can you hear those lovely sounds?

____

b Like the happy chirping of these crickets here on the ground …

____

c Even the trickle of water in that fountain over there.

____

Question 9

a Complete the following sentences with the appropriate demonstrative pronoun: *this*, *that*, *these*, *those*.

"I love listening to ______________ soothing sounds of the ocean."

"Can you please turn down ______________________ loud music?"

b Using all four demonstrative pronouns: *this*, *that*, *these*, *those*, write two sentences about the sounds you like and two sentences about the sounds you dislike.

Sounds I like:

i ____

____

____

____

Sounds I dislike:

ii ____

____

____

____

Question 10

a Re-read **Source 3** and then write a short paragraph describing a scene from nature, using at least three demonstrative pronouns.

____

____

____

____

____

____

b Imagine you are giving a tour of your school to a new student. Use demonstrative pronouns to point out different features of the school.

____

____

____

____

____

____

Part 2

Question 11

Imagine you are a scientist leading a workshop for young children. Explain how our senses of sight and sound work together to create a rich and meaningful experience of the world around us. Use examples from the provided sources to illustrate your points.

Your task:

- i Introduction: briefly introduce the idea of our senses working together.
- ii **Source 1** *Visualisation*: explain how our eyes capture and interpret light. Include details about the limitations of sight, like in darkness or with certain animals.
- iii **Source 2** *Vibrations*: explain how different types of sounds impact on us.
- iv **Source 3** *Sound or noise?*: Explain the importance of appreciating all kinds of sounds.
- v Conclusion: Summarise the importance of both sight and sound in understanding the world around us. Emphasise how appreciating these senses enriches our lives and helps us understand our environment.

Reflection

Answer these questions once you have completed the task.

- Make a list of three things in this task that you did well.

___

___

___

- What could you do better?

___

___

___

- Write down one thing that you learned in another task that helped you here.

___

___

___

Practice paper 6

This task has two parts. For both parts, you must read **Source 1** and **Source 2**.

- Part 1 has questions 1 to 6.
- Part 2 has question 7.

→ Before you start ...

Look at these students' responses for the following question: Who is your favourite Jamaican musical artist? Both students have the right answer, but Annika gets a better grade than Nadia. Can you see why?

Nadia's response	Annika's response
Sean Paul is cool because everyone knows his songs.	*My heart belongs to the Jamaican dancehall rapper, singer and record producer, Sean Paul. He captures the essence of Jamaican culture and society in a way that resonates deeply with me.*

Although both responses are correct, Nadia's response simply states a preference and provides a one-dimensional reason.

Annika's response, however, goes beyond the surface, explaining the connection between the artist's music and her personal experience or values.

Look at the instruction words and phrases in the Knowledge boxes below. Which Knowledge box goes with Nadia's and Annika's responses?

Write **Recalling information**, **Skills and concepts**, **Strategic thinking** or **Extended thinking** next to their name below. Think about what each instruction means in the Knowledge boxes before you answer the question.

Nadia ______________________ **Annika** ______________________

Recalling information	Skills and concepts	Strategic thinking	Extended thinking
Remember, recall, recognise or locate basic details and ideas. There is one correct answer.	Explain, show relationships; use your skills and what you know to make decisions about what to do and how to do it. There is one correct answer.	Explain your thinking and give reasons for your answers. There are different answers and different ways to find the answers.	Plan, think and put ideas together to solve a problem. There are many possible answers and ways of solving the problem.

Part 1

SOURCE 1

Sunshine Band

Remember that sinking feeling when your favourite band almost vanishes? Well, they are back! The new music of the Sunshine Band is like sunshine in song. It lifts you up and is perfect for healing a downhearted world.

Imagine sunshine, kids' giggles and summer breeze turned into music. That is this band. I first heard them stuck in traffic, frustrated and fuming. The radio blared their happy tune and, guess what? I sang my heart out, ignoring honks and stares. Like, who cares?

This music is pure joy, a summer breeze, a cure for all that ails you. Feeling deflated? Well, I already said it lifts you up, but it will also pump you up. World got you down? This will blast it away with pure joy.

In a world full of doom and gloom, this band opens the windows and lets the sunshine in. They remind us that even when it is dark, the sun still shines, ready to warm your soul and make you fly. So, turn it up, let the music wash over you and remember, when the world feels heavy, this band will always lift you up.

The following comments were posted on a website in response to the review in **Source 1**.

website comments SOURCE 2

1 minute ago
[1] **King:** This music is like someone is giving you a hug! It makes you want to dance, laugh and believe in brighter days.

3 minutes ago
[2] **RealityCheck:** While I appreciate the optimism, the world is not all sunshine and rainbows. Music should reflect the full spectrum of emotions, not just the happy bits.

5 minutes ago
[3] **MusicLover4Life**: This band is a gift! Dem sang ya mek yu waan sing alang, laff and fiiget bout yu worries. Keep spreadin di sunshine!

7 minutes ago
[4] **Chillin:** Not my usual jam, but I gotta admit, dis tune catchy. Good vibes fi sure, but I need a bit more spice in my music.

10 minutes ago
5 **SunshineSoul:** Dem bring di feel-good vibes back to music. Perfect fi road trip, beach chillin' or just pumpin' up di energy.

12 minutes ago
6 **OldSkool:** Respect the positive vibes, but I miss the raw energy and realness of their earlier stuff. Although this is okay, it feels a bit polished for my taste.

15 minutes ago
7 **Cool&thegang:** The music feels a bit repetitive. Maybe some more variety in the sound could keep it fresh?

17 minutes ago
8 **MelodyMaster:** The lyrics are sweet and positive, but perhaps too sentimental. Some will find the happy sounds pleasant, however, it is too mushy for me.

22 minutes ago
9 **Fusion:** I dig the positive vibes, but the sound feels too generic. They definitely need to produce something different to give them a unique edge.

Question 1

Find five different words or phrases from the **Source 1** article that clearly show the author's point of view.

ICT and Mathematics link: You could create an online survey using Google Forms or Microsoft Forms to find out your friends' and family members' favourite music genres or bands. Then, use the results to make a chart or graph.

Question 2

a Identify the following persuasive techniques that the author has used in **Source 1**.

Persuasive techniques	Example	Your answers
Repetition	"sunshine"	
Emotive language / appeals to emotions	"downhearted"	

A hyperbole is an exaggerated non-literal statement used in speech and texts to add emphasis. For example, "The new music of the Sunshine Band is like sunshine in song. It lifts you up and is perfect for healing a downhearted world". These sentences exaggerate the positive impact of the music by comparing it to sunshine and claiming it can heal the entire world.

b Identify three hyperboles in **Source 1**.

Question 3

Read the comments in **Source 2**. Compare and sort the language used into categories of positive, neutral and negative. The first one in each category has been done as examples.

Positive	Neutral	Negative
1, ______	4, ______	2, ______

Question 4

Read each statement in the table and place a tick [✔] to identify whether each one is supported by **Source 1**, **Source 2**, **Both sources** or **Neither source**.

Statement	Source 1	Source 2	Both sources	Neither source
Music can cure sadness.				
It is like sunshine and summer breeze.				
The melody is catchy.				
It has positive vibes.				
The emotional depth is striking.				

The past perfect tense is formed using **had** + the **past participle** of the verb. We use the past perfect tense to describe an event that happened before another in the past. For example, "By the end of the exam, I **had forgotten** my responses".

Question 5

a Choose the sentence that uses the past perfect tense correctly. Circle the answer.

i She had already eaten dinner when I arrived.

ii She ate dinner before I arrived.

iii She has eaten dinner after I arrived.

iv She eats dinner before I arrive.

b Which sentence correctly completes this sequence of events? Circle the answer.

"I went to the store. I realised I had forgotten my wallet."

i I had left my wallet at home.

ii I leave my wallet at home.

iv I will leave my wallet at home.

v I am leaving my wallet at home.

Question 6

a Fill in the blank with the correct form of the verbs.

i By the time the movie started, we ______________ already ______________ our popcorn. (have, eat)

ii I could not find my smartphone because I ______________ it in my other bag. (have, leave)

iii She was tired because she ______________ up all night studying for the exam. (have, be)

b Identify and correct the error in the use of the past perfect tense in this sentence:

"I had already went to the park when you called."

____

c Write two sentences using the past perfect tense to describe an event that happened before another event in the past.

____

____

____

____

d Write a short paragraph about a time when you were late for something. Use the past perfect tense to describe the events that led up to your lateness.

____

____

____

____

Part 2

Question 7

Write a story about a time when you had to overcome a challenge. Use the past perfect tense to describe your initial feelings, the obstacles you faced and the steps you took to overcome it.

Your story should demonstrate the following points:

- Relevance: it addresses the task and focuses on overcoming a challenge.
- Development: it unfolds logically, with descriptions of the initial situation, the challenge and the actions taken.
- Resolution: it has a satisfying conclusion that shows the character overcoming the challenge and reflecting on the experience.
- Structure: it has a clear beginning, middle and end. Paragraphs are used effectively to organise ideas.
- Past perfect tense: The past perfect tense is used effectively to describe events and actions that happened before another past event.

Reflection

Can you answer "yes" to all these questions? If not, write down what you need to do to change your answer.

- Did I understand all the questions?

- Did I know what to do to answer them?

- Did I follow the instructions correctly?

- Was my work clear and organised?